The New African Americans

Books About Immigrants and Immigration by Brent Ashabranner

The New Americans: Changing Patterns in U.S. Immigration
Children of the Maya: A Guatemalan Indian Odyssey
Into a Strange Land: Unaccompanied Refugee Youth in America
The Vanishing Border: A Photographic Journey Along Our Frontier with Mexico
Still a Nation of Immigrants
Our Beckoning Borders: Illegal Immigration to America
To Seek a Better World: The Haitian Minority in America
An Ancient Heritage: The Arab-American Minority

Other Linnet Books by Brent Ashabranner

The Choctaw Code
Dark Harvest: Migrant Farmworkers in America
The Lion's Whiskers and Other Ethiopian Tales

THE NEW AFRICAN AMERICANS

by Brent Ashabranner

Photographs by
Jennifer Ashabranner

LINNET BOOKS
1999

EB BR
J
E184
.A24
A84
1999

Text © 1999 by Brent Ashabranner
Photographs © 1999 by Jennifer Ashabranner
All rights reserved.
First published 1999 by Linnet Books, an imprint of
The Shoe String Press, Inc., 2 Linsley Street,
North Haven, Connecticut 06473.

Library of Congress Cataloging-in-Publication Data

Ashabranner, Brent K., 1921–
    The new African Americans / by Brent Ashabranner; photographs by Jennifer Ashabranner.
    p. cm.
    Includes bibliographical references (p.   ) and index.
    SUMMARY: Looks at Africans who have immigrated to the United States since the 1890s, examining who they are, why they came, how American laws work for and against them, and how they have fared.
    ISBN 0-208-02420-4 (lib. bdg. : alk. paper)
    1. Africans—United States Juvenile literature. 2. Immigrants—United States Juvenile literature. 3. Africa—Emigration and immigration—History Juvenile literature. 4. United States—Emigration and immigration—History Juvenile literature. [1. Africans—United States. 2. Immigrants. 3. Africa—Emigration and immigration. 4. United States—Emigration and immigration.]
I. Ashabranner, Jennifer, ill. II. Title.
    E184.A24 A84 1999
    304.87306–dc21   99-31388
                                                                                       CIP

The paper in this publication meets the minimum requirements of American National Standard for Information Sciences—Permanence of Paper for Printed Library Materials, ANSI Z39.48-1984. ∞

Designed by Sanna Stanley
Printed in the United States of America

*This book is for Muriel and Willis Branch
and for Missouri Virginia Miller*

Contents

	Author's Note	ix
I.	**African Immigration to America: A Brief Review**	
	The Kunta Kinte Festival	3
	The First African Immigrants	9
	African Immigration: 1865–1965	16
	A New Immigration Law for a New Era	19
II.	**Today's African Immigrants**	
	Who Are the New African Americans?	23
	Why Do They Come? Many Motives, One Goal	30
III.	**What Today's African Immigrants Bring to America**	
	For Cities and Suburbs: A Touch of Africa	47
	"America Means You Have to Discipline Yourself"	59
	Tales to Tell	64
	A Winning Team	73
IV.	**African Immigration to America Beyond the Year 2000**	81
	Additional Information About Africa	92
	Bibliography	103
	Index	105

Author's Note

For much of the twentieth century a small number of white Africans—principally from South Africa but a few from other African countries—have emigrated to the United States. Originally they or their ancestors came to Africa from England or elsewhere in Europe. These white immigrants from Africa have indeed become African Americans. In this book, however, I am writing only about black immigrants to this country.

All statistical figures about immigrants and immigration that I have used in this book are from the U.S. Bureau of the Census or the U.S. Immigration and Naturalization Service.

Some African words have accepted alternate English spellings. Ashanti/Asante and Ibo/Igbo are examples of such words. I have chosen the forms with which I have been most familiar through the years.

I wish to thank my good friend Stephen Chicoine for use of his photographs of the refugee Miller family in Houston and for information about the Millers. For the full story of the Miller family, read Steve's excellent book *A Liberian Family*; see my bibliography for details.

BRENT ASHABRANNER

I

AFRICAN IMMIGRATION TO AMERICA: A BRIEF REVIEW

Every year on a Saturday and Sunday in August, Africa comes alive on the campus of St. John's College in Annapolis, Maryland. The occasion is the Kunta Kinte Heritage Festival, a celebration of African, African-American, and African-Caribbean cultures. There is African drumming, hypnotic in its rhythm. There is African and African-American dancing. There is American jazz and African jazz. There are men, women, and children wearing the bright textiles of West Africa. More than anything, there are crowds of people, mostly African-Americans, but all other ethnic groups, too, enjoying the sights and sounds of the special days.

The Kunta Kinte Heritage Festival pays special tribute to the famed African-American author Alex Haley and to his powerful book *Roots.* In *Roots,* Haley traced the long life of his

THE NEW AFRICAN AMERICANS

great-great-great-great grandfather, Kunta Kinte, who was brought from Africa to America as a slave and given the name Toby. The ship carrying Kunta Kinte and ninety-seven other enslaved Africans arrived in the port of Annapolis on September 29, 1767. For more than a decade now, the annual Kunte Kinte Heritage Festival in Annapolis has commemorated that arrival.

Jennifer and I had attended the festival several years ago to help us get into the spirit of a book we were working on entitled *Still a Nation of Immigrants*. While we were writing and photographing this book, *The New African Americans*, it seemed a good idea to revisit the Kunta Kinte festival.

We went to the festival both days, and we were not disappointed. We watched West African folk dancing, listened to gospel singing and African jazz. Mainly we walked around, enjoying the day, looking at the wide range of African goods for sale: beautiful robes and dresses, children's clothes, woodcarvings, jewelry, baskets, pictures.

We talked to dealers from Africa. One, a West African whose name was Yao Loko, told us that he spends much of his time traveling throughout Africa looking for art and handicrafts. He comes to America once a year to sell at special events like this festival and to bring material for other dealers.

We talked to Hannah Chambers, a retired African-American schoolteacher and counselor, who lives in Annapolis. She was in charge of two interesting exhibits at the festival, both sponsored by her church. One exhibit explained Kwanzaa, the African-American celebration based on seven principles: unity, self-determination, collective work and responsibility, cooperative economics, purpose, creativity, faith. Kwanzaa comes from the East African

African dealer Yao Loko at the Kunta Kinte festival.

Hannah Chambers and her Gambia display at the Kunta Kinte festival.

Swahili word *kwanza*, which means "the first" or "the first fruits of the harvest."

Mrs. Chambers's other table was especially appropriate for the Kunta Kinte festival. It had a display board describing in words and photographs the West African country of The Gambia. ("The" is an official part of the country's name.) The Gambia is the smallest country in West Africa, a narrow strip of land on both sides of the Gambia River, which empties into the Atlantic Ocean. The Gambia is surrounded on the other three sides by Senegal, a large West African country.

It was to the region of the Gambia River that Alex Haley, through years of exhaustive research, traced his ancient ancestor,

An African dealer beautifully dressed for the festival.

Three young African Americans enjoy the Kunta Kinte Heritage Festival.

THE NEW AFRICAN AMERICANS

Kunta Kinte. Here Kunta Kinte had been born and raised, and it was from here that he was kidnapped and brought as a slave to Annapolis. All of that history Haley described in *Roots*. When Hannah Chambers first read *Roots* she was deeply moved by the story of Kunta Kinte. In 1997 she fulfilled a deep desire to visit The Gambia. She retraced Alex Haley's route down the river, and she visited the village where Haley's great-great-great-great grandfather had been born.

"It was wonderful," Mrs. Chambers told me, "and I talked to the oldest person in the village."

Late on Sunday afternoon while Jennifer was taking photographs, I wandered off to watch the Caribbean limbo dancers. In the seat next to me was a young African-American man. We talked a bit about the Kunta Kinte festival and agreed that it was well worth coming to. He told me that he was from Raleigh, North Carolina, and that he had been to all of the Kunta Kinte festivals since the first one in 1988.

"That's a pretty long drive," I said, calculating the distance between Raleigh and Annapolis.

"I guess," he said, "but not too far to get a feeling for your roots."

I thought about Alex Haley's twelve years of research and travel on three continents to learn about his roots.

"No," I agreed, "not a bit too far."

The First African Immigrants

The original thirteen colonies from which our nation grew were settled by immigrants from England and a few other European countries. After the colonial period, immigration from Great Britain continued to dominate, although German immigrants began to come in increasing numbers to the young nation that called itself the United States of America.

But almost from the beginning of colonization and well into the period of national growth, immigrants came to this new land from another part of the world, a little-known continent called Africa. They were immigrants in the sense that an immigrant is a person who comes to a country to take up permanent residence. Unlike Europeans, however, they did not come because they wanted to. The Africans came in chains and shackles—men,

THE NEW AFRICAN AMERICANS

women, and children—kidnapped from their homeland, torn from their families, and sold as slaves in the New World.

It is surely our nation's most bitter irony that at the same time millions of Europeans were drawn to America by the promise of greater political and religious freedom and unlimited opportunity to build a better life for themselves, hundreds of thousands of Africans were being transported across the Atlantic and forced into a life of hopeless slavery.

The transporting of enslaved Africans—largely from West and Central Africa—to the Americas was the largest forced migration in modern history. In the almost four hundred years of the slave trade, from the late fifteenth century to the late nineteenth century, more than eleven million Africans were brought to the New World. Millions more died during the horrible ocean voyages that usually took more than two months.

The largest number of Africans, over seven million, were taken to Brazil, a Portuguese colony, which did not abolish slavery until 1888. The second greatest number were taken to the British, Spanish, French, and Dutch-controlled islands of the Caribbean to work on plantations created to supply Europe's ever-growing taste for sugar.

About five hundred thousand Africans were sold into slavery in North America. The slave trade began there in colonial times with the arrival of a slave ship in Virginia in 1619 and lasted until the importation of slaves into the United States was outlawed in 1808. Even after the law's passage another thirty thousand or more Africans were smuggled into the country by illegal slave traders. The 1808 law did not give freedom to enslaved persons already in the country.

The First African Immigrants

When all else has been said, the unending quest for freedom and the establishment of human rights was the ultimate contribution of early African-Americans to the nation they were a part of.*

---

*To learn more about the contributions of enslaved African-Americans to the culture and traditions of America, I recommend the following books: *The Water Brought Us: The Story of the Gullah-Speaking People* by Muriel Miller Branch and *The Strength of These Arms: Life in the Slave Quarters* by Raymond Bial.

African Immigration: 1865–1965

The Civil War, which ended with the defeat of the Confederacy in 1865, brought to a close over two hundred years of slavery in North America. Africans could now immigrate to the United States as free persons. In the post–Civil War era there were no immigration laws; anyone, anywhere in the world, with the desire and the price of a boat ticket could come to America.

The rapid industrial development of America—coal mines, oil fields and refineries, steel mills, textile mills and factories, railroads, automotive plants—brought about an explosion of immigration from Europe, not only from northern and western European countries such as England, Ireland, and Germany, but also from Italy, Russia, Austria, and other southern and eastern European countries. The new American industries needed people, and European

African Immigration: 1865–1965

immigrants saw job and other economic opportunities that their countries could not offer.

In one ten-year period, 1881–1890, almost five million European immigrants came to America, more than twice the number of any previous decade. In that same period, fewer than one thousand immigrants came from Africa to America—a ratio of almost five thousand European immigrants to one African! There are many reasons historically why immigration to America should have been much greater from Europe than from Africa. But the tiny trickle of Africans to America in the years immediately after the Civil War clearly meant that, in the African mind, America was still seen as a place of slavery. Centuries of kidnappings and brutal raids by slavers on villages could not be erased in a few years. African immigration to South America, Central America, and the Caribbean was also minimal during this period.

After 1900 immigration from Africa to the United States began to increase as memories of slavery became less vivid. In the twenty-year period, 1901–1920, over fifteen thousand Africans immigrated to the United States. That was a mere drop compared to the twelve million Europeans who immigrated in the same period; still, it was evidence that a growing number of Africans were becoming interested in the possibility of starting a new life in America.

The growing interest of Africans in immigrating to the United States was dealt a serious blow in 1924 when Congress passed a highly discriminatory immigration law. The law, designed to favor immigration from northern and western European countries, limited Africa and Asia to only 2 percent of the number of persons allowed to immigrate to the United States each year. (The law did not restrict immigration from Canada, Mexico, Central America, or South America.)

This restrictive law stifled immigration from both Africa and Asia for the next forty years. During that four-decade period, 1924–1964, immigration from all African countries averaged fewer than one thousand persons a year. Immigration from Europe was reduced during those years by both the Great Depression of the thirties and by World War II but still averaged 150,000 a year.

A New Immigration Law for a New Era

World War II brought the United States into a closer relationship with the rest of the world and changed the way Americans looked at other countries and people. After the war many Americans began to question the racism and prejudice against certain nationalities that had become a part of U.S. immigration policy. President Eisenhower urged changes in immigration law to "get the bigotry out of it." President John Kennedy said that immigration quotas based on race and country of origin were "without basis in either logic or reason."

Because of the Vietnam War and the fight for civil rights waged by courageous African Americans, the 1960s were years of soul-searching for millions of Americans about social justice and human rights. In 1965 Congress passed and President Lyndon Johnson signed

THE NEW AFRICAN AMERICANS

into law a new immigration act which brought racial and ethnic quotas to an end. Although many changes have been made, this important piece of legislation remains the law of the land to this day.

The law is very complex with scores of provisions, but the most important ones are these:

— No person can be refused immigrant status to the United States because of race, nationality, or religion.
— The annual limit on immigration is set by Congress; it may change from year to year. (The limit in 1990 was 700,000 immigrants; in 1996 it was raised to 915,000.)
— Refugees from political or religious persecution who are admitted to the United States do not count against the regular immigration limit.
— Preferences in issuing immigrant visas will be shown for 1) family reunification—close relatives of U.S. citizens first and then of legally resident noncitizens; 2) persons with special occupational and professional skills that are needed in the United States.

The new law had an immediate effect on immigration from sub-Saharan Africa. In the one hundred years between the end of the Civil War and the Immigration Act of 1965, only sixty-five thousand African immigrants had come to the United States. In one ten-year period after the act's passage, 1987-1996, over three hundred thousand immigrants came from forty African countries.

In this new era of immigration an increasing number of Africans were seriously considering the possibility of becoming African-Americans.

II

TODAY'S AFRICAN IMMIGRANTS

Who Are the New African Americans?

A large majority of the approximately four hundred thousand Africa-born residents of the United States today have emigrated from English-speaking countries of West Africa, particularly from the former British colonies of Nigeria and Ghana. Since 1965, by far the largest numbers have come from and continue to come from Nigeria, the most populous country in Africa with 122 million people. In the ten-year period, 1987–1996, some fifty-five thousand emigrants left Nigeria to make their home in the United States. Ghana, with a much smaller population of about nineteen million, has a considerably higher emigration rate than Nigeria. In that same period, 1987–1996, more than twenty-five thousand people emigrated from Ghana to the United States.

Many of today's West African immigrants to the United States

Cape Verdean-Americans from Massachusetts and Rhode Island joined a group from Cape Verde in the Smithsonian Institution 1995 Festival of American Folklife in Washington, D.C. With centuries of influence from different parts of Africa and from Portugal, Cape Verdean musical traditions are rich. The morna, considered the Cape Verdean national form of song, stresses feelings associated with emigration: nostalgia for home, longing for family, friends, and lovers left behind.

have come from Liberia, a small country with a population of less than three million. Liberia was founded in 1821 by the American Colonization Society as a haven for freed American slaves; in time about fifteen thousand freed slaves were settled there. Because of its origins, Liberia has always had a special link with America. The Liberian flag looks much like the American flag. Monrovia, the capital city, was named for James Monroe, the fifth American

Who Are the New African Americans?

president. Many Liberian village signposts carry names such as Philadelphia, Memphis, and Charlottesville.

Unlike the English-speaking countries of West Africa, the French-speaking countries (former French colonies) such as Côte d'Ivoire (Ivory Coast), Senegal, and Guinea have seen only a few thousand of their citizens immigrate to the United States. Clearly, knowing English has been an incentive for Nigerian and Ghanaians to immigrate to America—and England. Many thousands have immigrated to Great Britain. French-speaking West Africans with a desire to immigrate have quite naturally tended to look toward France.

The most unusual immigration story in all of Africa is to be found in the small West African country of Cape Verde (pronounced "Cape Vurd"), which lies about 400 miles west of the African mainland. With approximately 400,000 people, mostly of mixed Portuguese and African ancestry, Cape Verde has the smallest population of any sub-Saharan African country. Yet an estimated 350,000 Cape Verdean immigrants and their descendants live in the United States today; over 60,000 Cape Verdeans have come to the United States since 1965 when increased immigration from Africa became possible under the new immigration law.

How could so many immigrants come from one tiny country? Portuguese explorers discovered the islands, at that time uninhabited, in 1460. Within a few years settlers from Portugal began to immigrate there. They grew sugarcane and cotton, planted fruit trees, and imported slaves from the African mainland to work the new plantations. For a time the islands prospered as a transshipment point for enslaved Africans being transported to the New World, but in the late 1600s the use of the islands by slavers declined.

THE NEW AFRICAN AMERICANS

Despite its name, which means "green," Cape Verde is a windy, brown land with a long history of severe droughts and famines. In order to survive many Cape Verdeans became fishermen. They also became excellent boatmen. Even before 1800 Yankee whaling ships were calling at Cape Verde ports for refueling and supplies. Cape Verdean men began to sign onto the ships' crews as a means of escaping the poverty of Cape Verde. They became well known for their skills and bravery and held many ship positions, including harpooner and ship's captain. By the 1840s over 40 percent of all Yankee ship crews were Cape Verdeans.

When the young Cape Verdean seamen saw the whaling areas of New England—Nantucket, New Bedford, Providence, and others—they saw a chance to escape the grinding poverty of Cape Verde and start a new life in America. There were no immigration laws at that time in the 1800s, and they came by the thousands and brought their relatives by the tens of thousands. Over the years the Cape Verdeans—now in their third, fourth, and fifth generations—have, like other immigrant groups, melded into the American culture while retaining elements of their original island culture. Cape Verdeans began life in America as textile workers, cranberry pickers, dockworkers, and whalers. Today many Cape Verdean-Americans are still in blue-collar work, while others have become teachers, doctors, nurses, lawyers, journalists, and members of other professions. Most still live in New England.

Outside of West Africa, the greatest number of African immigrants to America have come from Ethiopia, a large country in the eastern "horn" of Africa. With over fifty-eight million people, Ethiopia is the second most populous country in sub-Saharan

Who Are the New African Americans?

Africa. Immigration from Ethiopia, which reached its highest figure of 6,086 in 1996, has been spurred by years of terrible drought, fighting with neighboring countries, and internal political conflict. Unlike the English-speaking countries of West Africa, Ethiopia was never under British colonial rule; English, however, has been the language of instruction in Ethiopian secondary schools and universities for well over half a century. Many Ethiopians bring this language advantage with them to America. At the request of Emperor Haile Selassie, a great deal of educational assistance was given to Ethiopia by the U.S. foreign aid program in the 1950s and by Peace Corps volunteer teachers in the 1960s.

At least a few immigrants to America have come from each of sub-Saharan Africa's forty-eight countries, even from such small and little-known nations as Comoros (eleven immigrants since 1992) and Sao Tome and Principe (thirty-five immigrants since 1986). Other than the countries already mentioned, however, substantial numbers of immigrants to America have come only from Kenya in East Africa and from South Africa, about fifteen hundred annually from Kenya in recent years, about twenty-five hundred from South Africa. The latter figure includes both black and white South Africans.

One of the traditional pictures of immigrants to America is that of poor, uneducated, often illiterate "huddled masses" sailing past the Statue of Liberty in New York harbor to start a new life in "the land of the free." That picture is historically accurate for the late eighteenth century and the early decades of this century, but it bears very limited resemblance to the thousands of African immigrants arriving in the United States in the 1990s.

African immigrants are on the faculties of most major colleges and universities in America. Dr. Paa-Bekoe Henry Welbeck, an immigrant from Ghana, shown here with his wife, Elnora, is Assistant Provost for Information Technology at the College of William and Mary in Williamsburg, Virginia, and director of William and Mary Cable Television Programming. Dr. Welbeck and his wife, an art specialist, also own two stores that sell African goods.

Who Are the New African Americans?

Most of today's immigrants from Africa are poor. They probably have borrowed money or saved a long time to buy a ticket for their journey. They do not sail into New York harbor but instead land in a Boeing 747 at the international airports in New York, Washington, D.C., Houston, Atlanta, or Chicago.

But the typical African immigrant arriving in some U.S. city today is not uneducated and certainly not illiterate. One of the few positive legacies of decades of British and French colonial rule in Africa was good secondary schools and colleges, few in number but high in quality. According to a 1992 U.S. Census Bureau report entitled "The Foreign-Born Population in the United States," 88 percent of all of today's adult African immigrants have at least a high school education—a higher figure than adults born in the United States, which is 77 percent.

Forty-seven percent of all Africa-born adults in the United States have at least one college degree, compared to 20 percent of all foreign-born and 20 percent of all native-born adults. One in five Africa-born adults in the United States holds a master's or Ph.D. degree compared to one in fourteen for adults born in America.

Clearly, many African immigrants today bring a good education with them to America, and many more pursue further education after they arrive.

Why Do They Come?
Many Motives, One Goal

While immigration from Africa does not begin to match that from Latin America, Asia, and Europe, Africans are coming to the United States in increasing numbers—over fifty thousand in 1996, the highest African immigration in one year since the government began keeping records in 1820. Why do they come?

The traditional answer to that question is that all immigrants, no matter where in the world they come from, come to America to better themselves. That was true of immigrants in the past; it remains true of immigrants in the present. Bettering themselves can mean many things: escaping a brutal political regime; joining loved ones already in America; the chance to get a job and earn a decent wage; to pursue educational ambitions; to start a business; to find more opportunity for professional abilities and talents. One

Why Do They Come?

or more of those motives undoubtedly influenced all immigrants from Africa today.

Pursuit of education brings thousands of young African men and women to America every year. There are good colleges and universities in a number of African countries, but not nearly enough of them to meet the growing demand for higher education. Also, the African colleges are expensive to attend, and there is very little opportunity for students to find work to help pay their expenses.

In 1996 over twelve thousand African students were studying in American colleges and universities. Many African students come to America on scholarships provided by the U.S. foreign aid program or by private educational assistance organizations. Sometimes, however, scholarships meet only partial expenses, and many African students have to pay their own way entirely. There are few African students who do not work at one or more jobs—as taxi drivers, waiters, busboys, supermarket clerks, fast-food handlers—to survive as American college students.

Foreign students are not immigrants and are not counted as such in Immigration and Naturalization Service statistics. They come on student visas and are expected to return to their countries when their studies are completed. But studies often go on for years; the students become increasingly comfortable with living in the United States and begin to see career possibilities that would not be open to them if they returned to Africa. Some stay without permission after their student visas have expired; they are known as "visa abusers" and in fact are illegal immigrants. Most of the young African students who want to stay apply for legal resident status and most are approved. Under the immigration law they now qualify as persons with special occupational or professional skills that are needed in the United States.

Seth Borquaye's story is unusual in some ways, but it has much in common with the stories of thousands of other African students who have stayed to become productive citizens of the United States. Seth was born and raised in the capital city of Accra in Ghana. His parents were divorced, and Seth lived with his mother, four sisters, and a brother. Seth's mother owned a fishing boat. When they were not in school, Seth and his brother worked on the boat as part of the crew, fishing the Gulf of Guinea and the Bight of Benin.

"We caught lots of mackerel," Seth recalls.

Seth's mother was determined that her children get good educations. After secondary school, Seth earned a bachelor's degree in animal science at the University of Ghana in Accra. In 1981 he heard about a special six-month program in animal science at Louisiana State University. He applied to the university for a scholarship, received it, and departed for the United States on a student visa.

Study and life in America agreed with the young man from Ghana. While he was at LSU in Baton Rouge, Seth applied for admittance to the graduate school of Duquesne University in Pittsburgh. He was accepted as a graduate student, received an extension of his student visa, and traveled north to a climate far colder than he had known in Ghana or Louisiana. But he was immediately working too hard to be bothered by the weather. He had some scholarship help from Duquesne but not nearly enough to cover his living expenses. For three years he washed dishes in restaurants at night and learned the streets of Pittsburgh as a

Why Do They Come?

taxicab driver so that he could study and attend classes during the day. By 1984 he had earned a Master of Science degree in microbiology, but in his three years at Duquesne he had done much more than work and study. He had made two momentous decisions. One was to marry a young Ghanaian woman he had met in Pittsburgh. The other was to apply for U.S. citizenship. After the required five-year waiting period, Seth became an American citizen in 1988.

He also knew that he wanted to push on with his education. With his fine record at Duquesne, he was readily accepted into the University of Pittsburgh graduate program in public health and then into the university's School of Medicine when he decided that he wanted to become a medical doctor.

That decision proved to be fateful in another and quite unexpected way. In his second year of medical school, Seth learned of a U.S. Army program in which his school expenses would be paid by the army in return for a period of service at an army hospital or other army medical facility. He was a citizen now and could join the army, which he did in 1991 and was commissioned as a second lieutenant. When he graduated with his degree as doctor of medicine in May, 1994, he was promoted to captain.

Today Seth Borquaye, M.D., is on the medical staff at the William Beaumont Army Medical Center in El Paso, Texas. He is now a major. His plan, after he has completed his army obligations, is to join a group medical practice somewhere in the United States. And beyond that?

"Someday," Dr. Borquaye told me, "after perhaps ten years of practice here and I have accumulated some money, I would like to go back to Ghana and practice medicine there. It is where I am most needed."

Seth Borquaye, M.D., in his office at the William Beaumont Army Medical Center in El Paso, Texas.

Below: The Borquaye family. Left to right: Wife Adeline; Seth in military dress blues holding Amanda, age two; and Iris, age sixteen. In front is Yolanda, age six.

Why Do They Come?

Education is the driving force behind much African immigration, but it was not Elie Koukoui's motive for coming to the United States. He had completed his education before he ever set foot on American soil. Born and raised in the small but beautiful West African country of Benin—a French colony called Dahomey until it gained its independence in 1960—Mr. Koukoui had much of his schooling there and for a time taught French in an elementary school. He then went to the University of Abidjan in the neighboring country of Côte d'Ivoire, also a former French territory, where he took a degree in business administration.

Like many other Africans who have been raised and schooled in countries that were formerly under French rule, Elie Koukoui decided to go to France to explore career opportunities. Bilingual in French and thoroughly familiar with French customs, Mr. Koukoui was comfortable living in Paris, where he worked part of the time for Club Med, a large company in the overseas vacation field. But after three years in Paris, he had not found the kind of career opportunities he was looking for.

He decided to visit a friend in Washington, D.C., just to look around. He came with no serious thought of immigrating to the United States; but in looking around, he liked what he saw: the energy of the country, the basic friendliness of people, the way that immigrants of many nationalities found to get a foothold in business for themselves. Mr. Koukoui decided that he would come to America to live, and with his education and work experience, he was able to get a permanent resident visa.

With that decision, Elie Koukoui's story becomes an almost classic immigrant tale of hard work and determination to succeed.

THE NEW AFRICAN AMERICANS

Although fluent in French and his native Goun language, he knew almost no English, and he had to make a living while he learned still another tongue. He began as a busboy, clearing tables in a Holiday Inn restaurant in Washington. When he wasn't working, he studied English-language learning books, listened to the radio, and watched television, not for entertainment but to try to understand what the people on the shows were saying.

His knowledge of English grew quickly, and he soon graduated from busboy to waiter and then to headwaiter. His next move upward was a big one. With his increased English fluency, his newly acquired ground-level knowledge of the restaurant business, and his business administration university studies to recommend him, he became manager of the Holiday Inn restaurant.

For many people that would have completed an immigrant success story. But like untold numbers of immigrants before him, Mr. Koukoui wanted his own business, and he had an idea of how to get it. He had become aware of a growing interest in the United States in the arts, crafts, and textiles of Africa. He began by having his large family in Benin—fifteen brothers, sisters, and other relatives—send him things that they could buy in the capital city of Porto Novo and other parts of the country where they lived. They sent mostly small things, a few at a time: ebony statues, masks carved by Benin craftsmen, jewelry, robes and other clothes. When he had accumulated enough material, he began selling it at the Holiday Inn during his free time and days off from his restaurant management position.

Elie Koukoui has now been in the United States for eight years and no longer manages the restaurant at the Holiday Inn. His business, which he calls African-Expression Gallerie, keeps him busier

Elie Koukoui brings his business, African-Expression Gallerie, to the Kunta Kinte Heritage Festival.

than he has ever been before. He sells by appointment and at events such as the Kunta Kinte Heritage Festival in Maryland. Selling his African pieces takes him to many cities throughout the country. Once a year he goes to Africa and brings back many interesting things such as Ashanti chairs, stools, games, and large excellently cast reproductions of the famous Benin bronzes of an earlier era. He is now looking for a location in which to locate his gallery permanently.

Jennifer's and my book *Still a Nation of Immigrants*, published in 1993, was about immigrants from all over the world. In it I wrote about only one African immigrant, a Ghanaian whose name is Harry Opoku. Harry's motive for coming to America in the early seventies was to try to become a big-league professional soccer player. Harry was a gifted soccer player, a star defender on both his high school and college teams in Ghana. He quit college to play the sport internationally for three years. When a professional soccer team was formed in Washington, D.C., Harry came to Washington to try out. Harry was good, but the competition was tough, and he did not get a contract.

Harry liked living in the United States and was able to qualify for permanent residence. He went into the import-export business but could not raise the capital to make a success of it. He tried various jobs before becoming an employee of an industrial cleaning company in northern Virginia. Harry's high school sweetheart came from Ghana, and they were married in 1976. They have two children, a daughter whose name Zulema means "Sun Is Rising," and a son, Mondell, who was named for former U.S. vice-president Walter Mondale.

Why Do They Come?

Harry thought that soccer was no longer a part of his life, but he was wrong. Mondell, who either inherited or acquired some of his father's soccer skills, began to show promise at an early age. Watching his son play on a youth club team when Mondell was eleven, Harry saw that the team coaches could use some sound soccer advice. He asked if he could help and was enthusiastically welcomed. When Harry's soccer experience and coaching ability became known, other local teams asked for his help. Within the limits of his free time, Harry was happy to help and over the years has become a soccer guru for teams in different age groups. Harry has been commended often for his valuable community service, but his answer is always that he is enjoying himself thoroughly.

Seven years had passed since we first wrote about Harry and his family, so we decided to look in on them again. The continuing story is a happy one. Harry is approaching twenty years as a valuable employee of his industrial cleaning firm. He still coaches as much Little League soccer as he has time for. Harry's wife, Bernice, is a hospice nurse in northern Virginia. Their daughter, Zulema, was visiting Ghana when we talked with them, staying in touch with family in Africa. She is now working in a day-care center and plans to study child care in college. Their son, Mondell, graduates from high school this year. He is a soccer standout and several colleges have an eye on him for a scholarship. Mondell wants to go to college; he has a strong interest in both computer science and physical education.

As Jennifer and I agreed, we couldn't invent a better immigrant success story than the real-life story of the Opoku family.

According to U.S. congressional law, a refugee is a person "who is unable or unwilling . . . to return to his country because

Harry Opoku

Why Do They Come?

of persecution on account of race, religion, or political opinion." Under this law, people anywhere in the world who are persecuted for political, religious, or racial reasons can ask to be admitted to the United States. Congress sets an annual limit on the number of refugees who can be admitted to the country, however. In recent years it has been about one hundred thousand, and overwhelmingly they have come from the strife-torn countries of Central America, particularly El Salvador and Guatemala, and from Cuba and Haiti in the Caribbean. Because of the closeness of these countries to the United States, thousands pour in illegally and are often declared refugees or are given asylum. Because of the Vietnam War, the United States gave refugee status to hundreds of thousands of Vietnamese, Cambodians, and Laotians in the 1970s and 1980s, and many still come from the refugee camps of Asia.

Today millions of Africans have fled from their countries to escape ancient tribal hatreds and other political violence. They are living in squalid refugee camps in other African countries. The turmoil in Rwanda, Congo, Angola, Liberia, and Sudan is some of the worst in the world. But because the selection process is so slow and complicated and because so many refugees come from countries close to the United States, only a small number of Africans ever reach this country as refugees.

Francis and Pearl Miller and their five children are among the fortunate few. Until ten years ago the Miller family had a comfortable home in Monrovia, the capital of Liberia. The children were receiving good educations. Francis Miller worked as a radio technician—a local or Liberian employee—for the Voice of America, a

Francis and Pearl Miller in their Houston home. Courtesy of Stephen Chicoine.

radio network of the United States Information Agency with stations in many countries around the world.

In 1989, long-simmering political tensions in Liberia broke out in fighting between government and rebel military forces, and the fighting quickly turned into tribal warfare. Life in Monrovia became a nightmare with gunfire day and night and food almost impossible to find. By 1990 government troops were slaughtering civilians of the Gio and Mano tribes that were supporting the rebels. Although he had nothing to do with the fighting, Francis Miller is a Mano, and for that reason alone, his life was in mortal danger.

Late in 1990 the Millers escaped from Monrovia and made their way to the neighboring country of Côte d'Ivoire. Since Francis Miller had been a U.S. government employee in Monrovia, he

Four of the Miller children, left to right: Kau, Deazee, Augustus, and Thomas, on the porch of the family apartment. Courtesy of Stephen Chicoine.

THE NEW AFRICAN AMERICANS

hoped that the American Embassy in Côte d'Ivoire would help him and his family go to the United States as refugees. The months of waiting were hard. The Millers had to register as refugees to receive a small monthly food ration from the United Nations. Francis Miller tried to find odd jobs to make a little money to help support his family.

Finally, in September of 1992, the Miller family received approval for immigration to the United States. Today the Millers are building a new life in Houston, Texas. It has not been easy. They live in a crowded part of the city, in an apartment too small for them. It took time for the Miller children to make new friends, but they have made them.

Francis and Pearl Miller have risen to the challenge of raising their family in a strange land. The biggest problem has been making enough money to support them. Pearl went to school to earn a nurse's aide certificate and now works at a senior-citizen home. Francis works nights at a hospital; he is taking classes at a community college so that in time he can become a radiology technician at the hospital.

There is little time and never quite enough money, and sometimes they think longingly of their life in Monrovia before the civil war. But both Francis and Pearl Miller are sure that their decision to come to America was the right one.

III

WHAT TODAY'S AFRICAN IMMIGRANTS BRING TO AMERICA

For Cities and Suburbs: A Touch of Africa

Immigrants to America traditionally have settled in the large cities of the country. By early in the twentieth century, 75 percent of the residents of such cities as New York, Boston, Chicago, Cleveland, and Detroit were immigrants or their children. Immigrant concentration in cities has continued into the latter part of the century and has made a significant difference in this era of "urban flight." According to *BusinessWeek* magazine, census figures show that the ten largest American cities grew by 4.7 percent during the decade of the eighties. But without immigrants during that period the population of these cities would have shrunk by 6.8 percent.

Certain areas of many cities are now alive with small immigrant businesses: Korean greengrocers, Hispanic grocery stores,

THE NEW AFRICAN AMERICANS

Vietnamese restaurants, Salvadorean restaurants, and hundreds of immigrant-run dry cleaners, flower shops, tailor shops, convenience stores, and other businesses that can be opened with limited capital and lots of hard family work. Without the immigrant business boom, part of many American cities would have become empty shells and tax revenues would have withered.

Until ten years ago African immigrants had not joined the big-city business parade. With immigration from Africa in the seventies and early eighties a trickle compared to the steady stream from other continents, there was not a sufficient base for African immigrant businesses. Immigrant stores and cafes hope to draw customers from all ethnic groups, but they depend on enough people from their own part of the world to keep their businesses afloat.

With immigration from Africa picking up briskly in the mid-eighties and increasing in the nineties, African businesses sprung into vigorous life in some cities. The Adams Morgan area of Washington, D.C., has long been known as an Hispanic part of the city, and it remains very much Latino. But today in a four-block area along Eighteenth Street you will find that Abou Master Goldsmith has a fine-looking jewelry shop. Yawa Books and Gifts features African books and goods. There is Kubosa Afrikan Clothier, and there is the Exotic Ethiopian Mart. Paula's Imports and Bazaar Atlas features baskets, textiles, and many other African products.

Anyone with a taste for African food will have come to just the right place. Twenty years ago you would have been lucky to find one Ethiopian restaurant in Washington or in any other American city, for that matter. Today in Adams Morgan there are six Ethiopian restaurants with such names as The Lion's Den

A Touch of Africa

Ethiopian Restaurant, The Red Sea Restaurant, and Fasika's Ethiopian Restaurant. There are Ethiopian restaurants in other parts of Washington, D.C., and they are beginning to appear in a number of other citites around the country—Atlanta, Dallas, New York, New Haven, Los Angeles. Clearly the American taste has quickly grown to include the fiery Ethiopian stew called *wat*, made with chicken, beef, or goat meat, and eaten—without benefit of knife, fork, or spoon—with *injera*, a thin, spongy, slightly sour bread made with an Ethiopian grain called *tef. Injera* takes some getting used to, but when you do, *wat* doesn't taste quite right without it. You simply use the soft *injera* with your fingers to pick up the meat and vegetables of the *wat*.

As a newcomer, African cuisine faces tough competition from American, French, Italian, Chinese, Mexican, German, Indian, and other foods long entrenched in this country. Except for Ethiopian food, success has been limited, but other African restaurateurs are determined to get a toehold. The Bukom West African Restaurant in Adams Morgan features such specialties as okra soup and *moi moi*, made with black-eyed peas, eggs, sardines, and other ingredients.

The Ghana Cafe, also in Adams Morgan, has a big AKWAABA ("Welcome") on an outside board which also announces its menu. Some of the dishes are *fufu*, *nkatekwan* (peanut soup), and palm-nut soup with beef, chicken, fish, or goat.

I talked with Anthony F. Opara, the manager of The Ghana Cafe, and he told me that business was good. That night, he said, a large group of former Peace Corps volunteers who had served in Ghana were coming for dinner. They were hungry for the food they had learned to enjoy in West Africa.

A taste for Ethiopian food is making its way steadily across America. Zemam's Ethiopian Cuisine has made a place for itself in Tucson, Arizona, the land of tamales, enchiladas, and chiles rellenos.

The rhythms of Africa are very much a part of Adams Morgan now.

A very young doorman at the Ghana Cafe in Adams Morgan.

THE NEW AFRICAN AMERICANS

The Ghana Cafe has its own website: www.ghanacafe.com!

Instead of staying in the crowded capital, thousands of African immigrants have settled in the Maryland and northern Virginia suburbs, still densely populated but with better schools and safer streets. A majority of African immigrants go to Maryland where most of the area's native-born African Americans live.

"We consider ourselves African-American, too," said a Nigeria-born merchant who runs a textile store there.

In these Maryland and Virginia suburbs, small African-immigrant-owned businesses have blossomed since 1990: hair-braiding salons; tailor, dressmaking, and fabric shops; grocery and specialty stores. They cater primarily to African-immigrant and native African-American trade, but other people find their merchandise interesting and prices sometimes surprisingly good.

At least half a dozen small African food stores are within a few minutes' drive of Jennifer's apartment in Washington's northern Virginia suburb of Alexandria. Sometimes when I am there, I go to the Awash Market and Butcher Shop, named for the Awash River that runs through the Great Rift Valley of Ethiopia. I may buy some Ethiopian coffee or a package of *injera*, the bread I acquired a taste for when I lived in Ethiopia.

My favorite African store there is Weyone Foods. You know the moment you walk into the store what country the owners came from because the magazine rack near the cash register is full of newspapers filled with stories about Sierra Leone and journals such as *The Sierra Leonean*. The store has been expanding and can scarcely be called small anymore. I may buy some African red beans or "yellow-eyed" peas and, if feeling adventurous, may even get some coco-yam flour and try making *fufu*, a kind of dumpling

A Touch of Africa

eaten with stews in several West African countries. At the Weyone meat counter you can usually find smoked goat and African cuts of pork, beef, and fowl.

I had spoken briefly with the Weyone owners from time to time but knew them only as Tom and Florence. When I decided to put the store into this book, I asked Tom to write out his full name for me; I had assumed that it was a Sierra Leonean tribal name, perhaps Mende or Temne, and I wanted to get the spelling right. Tom took my notebook and pen, wrote his name, and handed them back. In a clear, strong hand he had written: Thomas S. Johnson.

Tom laughed when he saw the puzzled look on my face, and he said, "You know about Freetown, don't you?"

I did know about Freetown, the capital of Sierra Leone, and had, in fact, spent a few days there years ago. Tom's question solved my puzzlement about his name. In the late 1700s and throughout the first half of the 1800s, liberated slaves were brought from Nova Scotia, then from Britain, to start life anew in West Africa. In time about fifty thousand freed slaves came from Britain to the African colony that, for obvious reasons, was given the name Freetown. The returned Africans usually had no tribal ties in the Sierra Leone peninsula, and most of them spoke English. The descendants of the freed slaves became known as Creoles and their language, a mixture of English and different African languages, is known as Creole.

Tom's ancestors came from England to Freetown and brought the name Johnson with them. Tom told me that the family name of his wife, Florence, also Creole, is McCauley. They immigrated to the United States twelve years ago, and Tom began to study business administration at the University of The District of Columbia, but

Tom Johnson

he dropped out when he and Florence had a chance to take over the store they now own. The original owner was also an African immigrant, and Tom said he was "going crazy" with licenses, health inspections, fees, taxes, reports, and business forms. He wanted out. With his background in business administration, the red tape did not bother Tom, and they were able to work out a plan to take over.

I asked Tom what the name of their store means. "Weyone is a

A Touch of Africa

Creole word," Tom told me. And he added with a touch of pride, "It means `We Own It'."

For millions of Americans, both native-born and immigrant, a part of the American dream always has been to have their own small business. The "mom-and-pop" stores of Italian and Lebanese immigrants—most often small groceries, bakeries, and butcher shops—have become a part of the American fabric. Today many African immigrants, like Tom and Florence Johnson, are gaining their foothold in America by establishing a small business with limited capital and a great deal of family hard work.

How do they get their start? One way is by belonging to a savings club, of which there are many in all U.S. cities with large African immigrant populations. Other immigrant groups, particularly the Koreans, have savings clubs, but they have a special importance for the African immigrant entrepreneur who wants to start his own small business. Called *isusus* by Ghanaians and Nigerians, the clubs are made up of a small group of African immigrants, usually no more than ten, who each contribute an agreed-upon amount of money, perhaps $100, for a certain number of weeks.

Each member takes his turn in receiving the weekly pot and in time has the capital to help start a small business. The savings club forces the member to make enough and save enough for his weekly contribution. His personal honor is at stake. One larger savings club to which a number of Nigerian Ibos in the Washington area belong is called in the Ibo language *Onye Aghakabwaneya Mbaise*. The English translation is "Let Nobody Leave His Brother Behind" Association.

Another way in which African immigrants slowly build a

Among the growing Richmond Ghanaian-immigrant population is the Biney-Amissah family. Thomas Biney-Amissah is a senior staff member of a Richmond jewelry manufacturing company. Naana Biney-Amissah is a reading specialist at an elementary school near Richmond.

nest egg is through sheer hard work, often holding two jobs at once, and through every member of a family, who is old enough and able, working at least part time. Service-industry jobs—taxi drivers, security guards, health care assistants, parking garage attendants, supermarket clerks and cashiers, fast-food workers—are excellent for part-time opportunities and for holding one job in the daytime and another at night. Because of their language facility, English-speaking Africans find unlimited opportunities in the service industries.

After posing for the family picture, Elizabeth, Albert Jeffery, and Theodora needed only a minute to get into their everyday clothes. Although born in America, each child has a Ghanaian name: Maame Esi Kumah (Elizabeth); Nana Kweku Prempeh (Albert Jeffery); and Ekua Boah (Theodora).

THE NEW AFRICAN AMERICANS

In the past three years I have taken taxis in Detroit, Houston, and Washington, D.C. On two of the rides my driver was a Nigerian, on the other a Ghanaian. In each of these cases their second "job" was college. They were all taking courses during the day, driving at night. In his fine book *The Other Americans: How Immigrants Renew Our Country, Our Economy, and Our Values*, Joel Millman cites the case of more than fifty Nigerians working at just one New York hospital.

For many workers, service-industry jobs are a dead-end road. African immigrants see them as a stepping-stone to better things.

The Washington, D.C.–area pattern of African immigrant business enterprise is replicated, with some variations, in other cities with large African immigrant concentrations such as New York, Houston, Detroit, and Atlanta. In some smaller cities the African immigrant population is growing steadily. Richmond, Virginia, for example, now has a Ghanaian business and professional association with more than one hundred members. African immigrant–owned textile and clothing boutiques and other specialty shops are no longer rarities but can be found in many cities across America.

"America Means You Have to Discipline Yourself"

Immigrants bring to their new lives in America a world of different backgrounds and experiences, but all successful immigrants I have met have brought two special qualities. One is a deep-down belief that America is still a place where they can build a good life. The other is being ready to work as hard as necessary to achieve that good life.

"We grew up with the idea that America is a magic place," a Jamaican immigrant once said to me. "When we get here, we find out that what we believed is true. But we learn that we have to make the magic happen ourselves, through hard work."

If the essence of immigrant success in America has ever been said more clearly than that, I haven't heard it.

THE NEW AFRICAN AMERICANS

Chuck Iweogu came to America from Nigeria in 1978 believing that he could make a good life for himself and ready to work hard to do it. His first name is not Chuck, of course, but rather Okechukwu, an Ibo name which means "God's Creation." By lifting the "chuk" out of the middle of Okechukwu and adding a *c*, he could have the familiar American nickname for Charles when he entered Texas Southern University in Houston.

Chuck chose Texas Southern because he had visited an uncle who was enrolled there, and he liked what he saw. TSU always has many African students enrolled, and Houston is a big friendly city with a large Nigerian immigrant population and a warm climate. Chuck had a Nigerian public school certificate and was working for the Bank of Nigeria when he applied for admission to TSU; he was readily accepted. With a large and caring family and a relatively good job, Chuck knew that he was leaving much behind in Nigeria. But he was young. He wanted to try his wings. He felt sure there was a good future for him in America.

Building on his Nigeria experience, Chuck studied banking and finance at Texas Southern. His father was a businessman doing contract work for the Nigerian government, and he helped finance Chuck's studies. To make the rest of the money he needed, Chuck worked for a food company that made deliveries to businesses and private residences in the Houston area. Chuck drove a delivery truck and worked in the warehouse.

Chuck graduated in 1983 with his degree in finance and banking and went to work for Kentucky Fried Chicken as an assistant manager. The reason he took the job was that he understood that he would become an auditor for KFC, work in which he would be

You Have to Discipline Yourself

using his finance background. But for reasons he isn't sure about, the auditing assignment never came. Months were passing, and he was not getting on with what he wanted to be his career. No other opportunities came along.

"I was very despondent," Chuck told me. "I thought every day about going back to Nigeria. I thought that might be the best thing to do."

From having talked with hundreds of immigrants, I am sure that such a time of discouragement comes to almost all of them. It may come many times during their years of finding their place in their new country. Some will give up and return to the country they came from. But most will stay and find their place in America.

Chuck Iweogu stayed. A friend from Washington, D.C., convinced him that he should try his fortunes in that city, and he moved there in the mid-eighties. He was determined to find his place in the field of finance, but while he did that he had to make a living. He went to work for Orkin, the pest-control company, and, after going through their sales training program, established a good sales territory in Maryland. He then went to work for Circuit City in sales. He was very successful in selling electronic equipment, one month reaching a record $100,000 in sales.

But he kept his mind on his goal, and persistence paid off. In time Chuck became associated with a mortgage-lending company in Maryland and had a chance to use his background and training in banking and finance. From there he went on to his present position as vice president in the Strategic Alliance Funding Company, a mortgage bank. Chuck works as a financial analyst, helping clients make decisions about buying, selling, and refinancing homes and other property.

The Iweogu family in front of their Washington, D.C., home. Chuck returned to Nigeria to be married. His wife is Ibo, as he is. Her name, Uche, means "Thought." Favour, their five-year-old daughter, also has an Ibo name, Ogochi, which means "God's Eagle." They are holding their five-month-old twins.

You Have to Discipline Yourself

I once asked Chuck what he thought were the ingredients of immigrant success in America. "You have to be willing to work hard, of course," he said. "Everyone knows that. You have to keep your eyes on your goal. It's easy to settle for something else. It's easy to get sidetracked. There are a million things to distract you in America. It's hard not to spend too much time on junk TV, video games, watching sports, nightclubs. You name it."

He thought a moment and then said, "America means you have to discipline yourself."

Tales to Tell

African cultures have some of the richest oral traditions to be found anywhere in the world. I became aware of that fact in the 1950s when my colleague, Russell Davis, and I collected hundreds of Ethiopian folktales and folk histories to be used in Ethiopian Ministry of Education schoolbooks. Russ and I later put some of the stories we especially liked into a book called *The Lion's Whiskers.*

I will always remember the explanation an old Ethiopian storyteller once gave me about folk stories and storytelling. "A good storyteller knows that you must like his stories," he said, "or you will not come again to listen. He also knows that you must sometimes learn something from his stories or you will soon know that they are not worth listening to."

Muriel Miller Branch, a native-born African American who lives in Richmond, Virginia, is both author and professional storyteller. She is a member of the National Storytelling Association.

For hundreds of years enslaved Africans brought stories of their tribal cultures to America, and many have become a part of our culture. Often African tales took on a new look as they were adapted to an American setting, but the stories retained their African core. Slavery itself produced a body of stories. A favorite theme was of the clever slave who always found a way to outwit his slightly stupid master.

A number of outstanding African-American writers such as Langston Hughes, Zora Neale Hurston, and Arna Bontemps pioneered in collecting and preserving African and African-American stories told in America. For a long time the African-American oral tradition, the storytelling art, was at a low ebb, but in recent years it has burst into new life with talented storytellers captivating audiences all over the country. A vigorous Association of Black Storytellers has been active since 1984.

Many African immigrants bring with them to America the traditional stories that they heard as children in their countries, and among today's immigrants are a few who are making a major contribution to the appreciation and understanding of African and African-American stories and storytelling.

One of these is Dr. Raouf Mama, Associate Professor of English at Eastern Connecticut State University in Willimantic. Raouf was born in the West African country of Benin, a member of the large Fon ethnic group. He grew up in the town of Allada, the cradle of the Fon civilization, and still rich in Fon culture. Raouf remembers an old saying that when a Fon king died, "He went to Allada."

Raouf also remembers that from an early age he heard colorful stories of kings and queens, trickster animals, princes and princesses, and magic drums. "After the evening meal we'd gather in the courtyard and listen to the adults tell stories," Raouf recalls. He remember that the stories were fascinating, sometimes exciting, sometimes scary, and he adds, "Invariably they had lessons: respect for the elderly, reverence for God, the importance of hard work, and the perils of greed and laziness."

Benin was at one time a French colony, and although Benin has been independent since 1960, French remains the language of instruction. All of Raouf's schooling, both elementary and secondary, was in French. But at age fourteen, when he was at the lycée (a secondary school which prepares students for university study), he had a course in English.

Tales to Tell

"I fell in love with English," Raouf told me.

Raouf graduated from the lycée as a top student and went to the University of Benin. His program of study, or major, at the university was English. His favorite teacher was a visiting professor from England. Raouf remembers that he often went to the professor's house to study and talk.

After earning his bachelor's degree at the University of Benin, Raouf received a scholarship to study at the University of Michigan in America. He received a master's degree in English and linguistics from Michigan in 1985 and then studied for his Ph.D., also at Michigan. He received his doctorate in 1990. His dissertation subject was "Images of Africa and Africans in Western Literature."

Raouf had long been aware that the rich oral traditions of Benin were in grave danger of permanent loss because they were not being recorded, a danger that in varying degrees every African country still faces. It was during his doctoral studies that he resolved to embark on a major project for the preservation of Beninese folktales, a project that has carried on beyond the awarding of his Ph.D. degree.

Over a six-year period, with the help of grants from the University of Michigan and other institutions, Raouf returned to Benin to record the traditional stories of Fon storytellers who ranged in age from ten to sixty. Additional years of translating the tales and polishing them led to the first offspring of a ten-year effort, a book entitled *Why Goats Smell Bad and Other Stories from Benin*. The book is a fascinating collection of twenty traditional folktales that makes the Fon culture come alive. The stories are grouped into four categories: Orphans, Twins, and Other Children; Cautionary Tales and Spirit Stories; Animal Wisdom; Trickster Tales.

Raouf Mama. Courtesy of Linnet Books

Why Goats Smell Bad was widely praised by book reviewers. And as Dr. Mama says in the book's introduction, "These tales tell the timeless story of how people the world over suffer, how they are delighted, and how they may triumph." He also points out that because the part of West Africa now called Benin was a major participant in the slave trade, "Fon culture is shared to a greater or lesser extent by black people in the United States, Brazil, Cuba, Haiti, and other Caribbean countries."

Tales to Tell

In one of our talks Raouf told me that when he meets and gets to know a U.S.-born African-American, "I see a brother or a sister."

Raouf's wife, Cherifath, is also of the Fon ethnic group. Raouf keeps the family storytelling tradition alive by telling folktales to his two daughters, ages four and nine. Twin sons are just over a year old but will soon be part of the family storytelling group.

The Mamas are a three-language family. Raouf and Cherifath speak English to the children but usually communicate between themselves in French or Fon. "It still feels a bit strange to speak English to my wife when we are by ourselves," he said.

Today at Eastern Connecticut State University, Professor Mama teaches courses in composition, introduction to literature, African literature, and, on occasion, storytelling. He also does public storytelling and lectures on the art of storytelling.

He did not say so, but I am sure Raouf is working on his next book of folktales.

THE ANT AND THE TOWER TO GOD

A folktale from *The Lion's Whiskers and Other Ethiopian Tales*. This is a story about the danger of vanity and self-importance and carries the subtle message that even the humblest of God's creatures (meaning people) have a right to be heard.

A great baboon king once ruled over the land of baboons with such wisdom and justice that all baboons loved him greatly. Even the smaller and less intelligent creatures loved the baboon king. They wanted him to be their king, too. But the baboons would not permit this.

"Why do ants and worms and other little things need a wise baboon as their king?" they asked. "They are not great animals. This is our king."

After many years the king grew old and sick and finally died. All of the baboons wept and wailed at the loss of their great king. But they forbade other animals to weep for him.

"He was our king," they told the others. "Only we have a right to cry for him."

The baboons gathered to have a great funeral feast. All the baboon chiefs gave speeches praising the virtues of their departed leader. After much crying and more speeches, one chief rose and said, "We must do something wonderful for our great king. His memory must be held high. What is the greatest honor we can pay him now that he is dead?"

One wise old chief answered, "We can take his body directly up to God. That would be a great honor."

"How can we do that?" the others asked. "God is in heaven. How can we get up there?"

"If we all work together very hard, we can do it," the old baboon said. "Anything is possible for creatures who have hands. We can build a tower to God."

The baboons set to work to build their tower to God. But everything they used to build the tower crumbled. The wood split, and the stones tumbled down. The wise old baboon said, "We must put ourselves into this. Other things will not do. We must bring all of the baboons of the world together. Then we can build a tower to God with our very bodies. One baboon can get on the back of another, and so on until our baboon tower reaches to heaven."

The baboons from all the world were gathered. They climbed, one on top of the other, and the tower began to reach up toward heaven.

Now a small ant had been traveling from a distant land to mourn for the king of the baboons. He had not heard that this was forbidden to small creatures. The ant arrived at the place where the baboon tower was almost built. The ant tried to call up to a big baboon who was about to climb up and form the top of the tower. He wanted to ask how he could join in the mourning.

"Sir," the ant called. "Sir, one moment, please."

But the big baboon ignored him. The baboon felt very important. He was going to form the top of the tower. He did not have time for a silly little ant.

The ant walked over to the wise old baboon who was supervising the building of the baboon tower. "Sir," the ant cried, to try to get his attention.

But the wise old baboon was too busy to talk to him. "Climb! Climb!" he called to the last baboon. "We are almost up to heaven."

Finally, the ant walked over to the base of the baboon tower. He saw the feet of the great baboon who formed the base of the tower. The baboon was a huge and powerful fellow who held up all the other baboons on his shoulders. The ant knew that his own little voice would not carry up to this mighty baboon.

So, to get the attention of the huge baboon, the ant stung him on the foot. The baboon gave a great cry and a great jump, and the whole tower crumpled and fell to the ground with a crash.

As baboons tumbled down all around him, the ant said as loudly as he could, "I came to tell you that I am sorry about the death of your great king."

Woodcut by Helen Siegl. Courtesy of Linnet Books

A Winning Team

"I am a businessman," Sam Achuko said to me the first time I met him.

Looking around his store in the upscale Landmark Mall in northern Virginia, I had no doubt that he is a businessman and a good one. The store, called Kelechi African Authentics, is full of African artifacts, African clothes and textiles, African jewelry, handbags, walking sticks, stools and hassocks, and hundreds of gift items of African origin. And I knew that Sam and his wife, Olivia, who is co-owner, have another store, also called Kelechi African Authentics. That one is in L'Enfant Plaza, one of the choicest locations in Washington. Sam is proud of the fact that their stores have beautiful things from every part of Africa, not just from West Africa.

Sam Achuko in one of the Kelechi stores.

What I did not know until I got to know Sam better and until I met Olivia is how much more than a businessman Sam is and what a winning team they make together. They are both from Eastern Nigeria, both of the Ibo ethnic group, but they did not know each other in Nigeria. Sam came to America first, arriving in Washington, D.C., in 1979, completely focused on getting a university education and, he thought at that time, becoming a lawyer.

Sam inherited a strong belief in the value of education from his parents who, he once told me, sold their land, even their clothes, to see that their children had a good education. When Sam

A Winning Team

arrived in America, he carried on that family tradition. He enrolled in Southeastern University in Washington and earned an undergraduate degree with a double major, one in accounting, the other in legal studies. After that he earned an MBPA, a master's degree in business and public administration. To pay his way in school, Sam at various times drove a taxi, worked at a Roy Rogers restaurant, and was a security guard at a motel.

Olivia Awusah, born and raised in the Eastern Nigerian village of Mbaise, received her secondary-school certificate at the age of sixteen, which was quite unusual, and decided immediately that she wanted to further her education in America. With the help of a sister who had immigrated to Detroit, Olivia flew to that city and, although still sixteen, was readily accepted as a student at Mercy College. The year was 1981.

She began her studies as a premedical major, but in her second year she met a friend of the family who was a chemical engineer. The more she learned about chemical engineering, the more excited she became. Remembering that time of discovery, she says, "Imagine taking a tree trunk and turning it into beautiful white paper!"

Olivia began researching universities with good chemical engineering programs and decided on Howard University in Washington, D.C. She applied for admission, was accepted, and moved to Washington in the summer of 1984. From the beginning, she was on her own financially. She was able to get an educational grant and a student loan, but they only partially covered her school and living expenses. To make up the difference Olivia took a housekeeping job in an apartment complex in exchange for her board and room. And to save seventy-five cents for lunch she made the long walk to and from the university every day instead of taking the bus. Difficult courses in chemical engineering and a time-consuming job all added up to a big load for a twenty-year-old Nigerian girl still learning her way around in a new country.

And then a very nice thing happened. Olivia made friends with another Nigerian girl who lived in the housing complex, sharing an apartment with her brother Samuel. Her name was Blessing Achuko, and she was also a student at Howard University. Blessing's brother, named for the biblical Samuel but known to his friends as Sam, had recently graduated from Southeastern with his master's degree and was now driving a taxi while he studied for law school entrance exams. When Blessing introduced Olivia to Sam, he invited Olivia to ride along in the taxi when he dropped his sister at Howard University each day. What a treat!

In time, with the approval—indeed the encouragement—of Blessing and Sam's elder sister, Charity, who was visiting from Nigeria, Sam and Olivia began a courtship. In the beginning Olivia was not sure that courtship and marriage were good ideas. Her chemical engineering program was very demanding, and she wanted to keep focused on it.

In time, however, her university studies were what brought them more closely together. Olivia was soon aware that Sam was genuinely interested in her education and that he encouraged and supported her in every way he could. With her own family thousands of miles away, she needed that encouragement. Their courtship began in late 1985, and they were married in 1986. She was now Olivia Achuko.

Their first child, a daughter, was born while Olivia was still a student at Howard. At first she was depressed, thinking that her

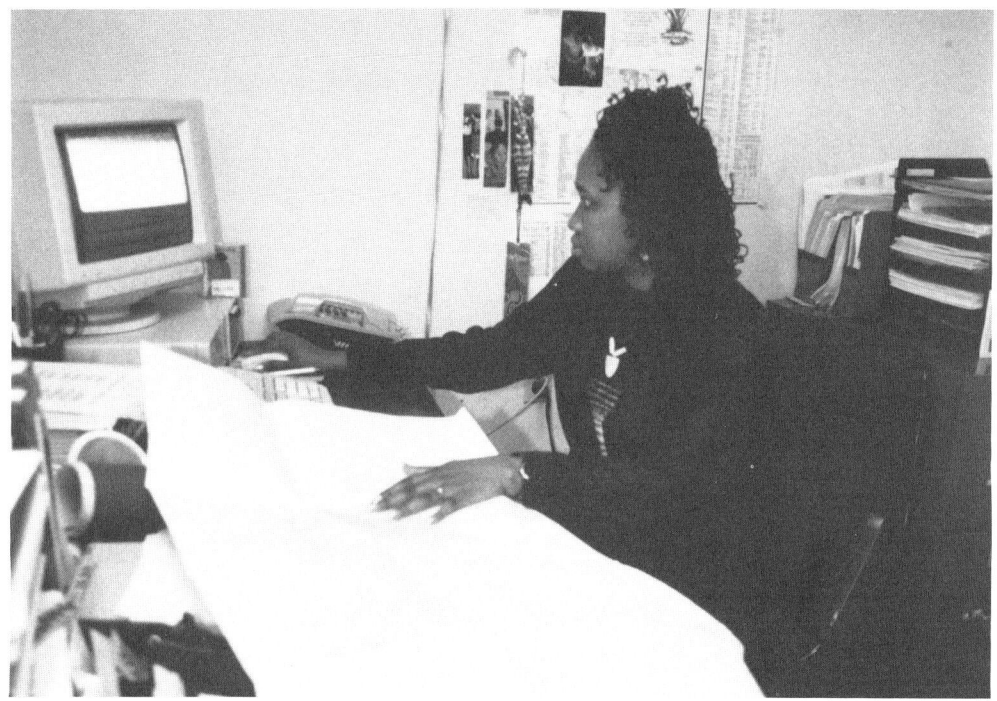

Olivia Achuko at work as an environmental engineer for the District of Columbia government.

university study and her career plans had ended. But Sam encouraged her to go on, and he was making enough money so that she could concentrate on her studies. She was back in her classes in less than a month after having the baby, and she graduated as a chemical engineer in 1988.

Today Olivia is employed as an environmental engineer for the District of Columbia government. Her primary responsibility is to monitor air quality in the city of Washington. She advises businesses that have a potential for polluting the air—such as gas stations, laundries, and cleaning establishments—what they must do to comply with clean-air standards. She also reviews all applications for construction of businesses or operation of equipment that might cause air pollution in the District. Olivia is putting her years of chemical engineering study to good use.

THE NEW AFRICAN AMERICANS

Sam and Olivia worked together to start their Kelechi African Authentics stores. With their family growing—the Achukos have four children—and Sam still contemplating law school, they felt the need of additional income. Their beginning in selling African materials was quite modest, as were their financial resources. At the church the Achukos attend some of the women frequently admired the beautiful African clothes that Olivia wore. That gave Olivia an idea. If women admired the clothes that much, why wouldn't they buy them if they had a chance?

Sam and Olivia took $700 of their meager savings and sent the money to Olivia's sister in Nigeria with instructions about what kind of clothes to have made with the money. In time Olivia's sister sent the clothes, one big suitcase full. That was the beginning. They sold the clothes quickly and sent money for more.

Sam was becoming increasingly aware of the growing interest of Americans in African art, artifacts, and materials of all kinds. He began to buy carefully and to sell from their house, along with the clothes. After a while he was able to make arrangments to sell from a kiosk or booth in the open area of Landmark Mall. The mall management thought that Sam would last only a few days, but their were wrong. And when they saw how well Sam was doing, they offered him store space inside the mall itself. Sam has always been grateful to the mall managers for their confidence in him.

Kelechi African Authentics was born, and it has grown and expanded. Sam Achuko put away his thoughts of being a lawyer and instead became what his studies at Southeastern University had prepared him to be: a very good businessman.

For all of his focus on business, Sam has a strong social conscience. He firmly believes that Americans, and particularly African

The Achuko family. The children's names all have religious meanings. From left to right: Chigozie, 12 ("God's Blessing"); Kelechi, 5 ("Giving Glory and Thanks to God"); Ogechi, 9 ("God's Time Is the Best"); Chibuike, 6 ("God Is Great and Powerful"). Standing next to Sam in back is Emmanuel Awusah, Olivia's nephew.

Americans, should know more about Africa and African cultures. He frequently speaks on these subjects at schools, army bases, and on public educational television and radio. He has received many awards and certificates of appreciation for his public service, a few of which he proudly displays in their stores. Sam and Olivia also take part in a number of charities in Fort Washington, Maryland, where they live.

The last time I visited Sam in his Landmark store, several

THE NEW AFRICAN AMERICANS

young African Americans stopped by from time to time to see him. Sometimes they talked laughingly, sometimes seriously. It was clear that they all had a great respect for Sam. At one point Sam said to me, "I tell them everybody can fly, but they have to learn how. That means education, hard work, and not getting discouraged."

And that, I thought, was a very good description of the winning team of Sam and Olivia Achuko.

IV

AFRICAN IMMIGRATION TO AMERICA BEYOND THE YEAR 2000

America began and grew as a nation of immigrants.
As we enter the twenty-first century, immigration continues to be a significant part of our national life, with newcomers each year now reaching the historic high figures of the late nineteenth and early twentieth centuries. While some American groups and individuals have always wanted less immigration, a deep-seated American belief has persisted that much of our strength as a nation comes from being a union of so many diverse races, ethnic groups, and cultures.

"Immigration is as American as apple pie" proclaimed a *Washington Post* Fourth of July editorial a few years ago. That statement would be difficult to argue with, and one of the main questions for the coming century is this: How will the pie be divided?

Peter Pipim is educational specialist for the Smithsonian Institution National Museum of African Art in Washington, D. C. The Museum has an outstanding collection of African tribal art and artifacts and puts on programs about African art and culture for school, college, and other groups. Mr. Pipim, shown here in a storytelling session, came to America from Ghana in 1969 and has been with the Museum since 1976. He is wearing the traditional cloth of the Asante people and is holding a doll called akau ba. The akua ba is carried in the back of the waist cloth by young Asante women as a charm to insure having beautiful children. This practice is declining, but continues in some Asante areas.

For the past twenty-five years by far the largest pieces of the pie have gone to Latin America (44 percent) and Asia (37 percent). Of the remaining 19 percent of annual legal immigration, only a tiny 3 percent slice has gone to Africa. A single statistic dramatically points up this difference in the volume of immigration: In the ten-year period, 1987–1996, a total of 311,000 immigrants came to the United States from *all* African countries. In that same ten-year period, 452,000 immigrants came from *one* small Asian country: Vietnam.

Another set of figures is equally revealing. In 1996, 12,000 African students were studying in the United States. That same year 31,000 students from South America, 90,000 from Europe, and 246,000 from Asia were studying in this country on student visas.

Beyond the Year 2000

Students are not immigrants, but, as we have seen, many who come to complete their education in the United States do not return to their countries. Because of their education and skills, they are able to secure a permanent resident visa or an employer-sponsored immigrant visa.

Compared to the rest of the world, why do so few Africans immigrate?

I once asked the minister-counselor of a West African country embassy that question. He had been a diplomat in Washington for a number of years and had thought a great deal about immigration. He talked first about the family reunification clause of U.S. immigration law that favors Latin Americans, Asians, and Europeans over Africans. The law gives preference to immigrant applicants with close relatives in the United States who are citizens—either native born or naturalized—and who will sponsor them as immigrants.

"Europeans and Latin Americans—especially Mexicans—have been coming to the United States in large numbers for so long," he said. "They have millions of brothers, sisters, parents, and other close relatives living here. So do Asians because so many came from Vietnam, Cambodia, and Laos as refugees after the Vietnam War. Many Chinese came as refugees from Communism. Africans have thirty million distant relatives in America, thirty million black Americans with the same ancestral roots as theirs, but not many brothers, sisters, parents, or children. So not many Africans qualify under the family reunification rule. Somehow that does not seem quite fair to me."

The minister-counselor thought for several moments before he spoke again. "I do not think there will ever be a flood of immigrants from Africa," he said, "even if immigration regulations permitted.

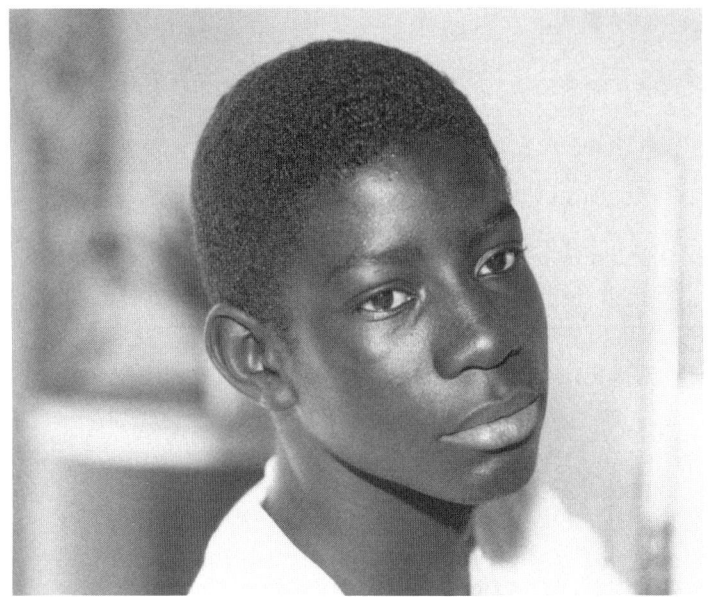

Nya Miller, whose family is shown on pages 42–43. Courtesy of Stephen Chicoine.

Longing for home, for family and friends left behind, is a part of almost all immigrant lives. Some cannot deal successfully with this homesickness and return to their native country, but most adjust, make new friends, and find their place in what at first is a strange new world. Jocelyne Kouabena, an immigrant from Côte d'Ivoire in West Africa, left a large family and the friends of a lifetime when she came to Ameria. Her husband is also a Côte d'Ivoire immigrant. Both have returned to Côte d'Ivoire to visit family and steep themselves in the culture in which they grew up. But they have returned to the U. S., have bought a house in Maryland, and are sure that their future is in America.

Right: Flavio Monteiro, a refugee from Angola, was separated from his family during the terrible civil war in that Central African country. Because his father was being hunted by government troops, Flavio fled to South Africa, where he nearly starved as a homeless street boy. He stowed away on an American merchant ship and, when found, was turned over to immigration authorities in New Orleans. He was granted political asylum and sent to Houston to live in Casa Juan Diego, a Catholic haven for children and others with immigration problems. Courtesy of Paul S. Conklin.

Left: Born in the East African country of Malawi, Mwiza Munthali became an immigrant somewhat by accident. At the age of nine, he accompanied his father to Washington, D.C. In time, his father returned to Malawi to live, but Mwiza stayed in America and went to the University of Iowa. Today he is an information specialist for the TransAfrica Forum, an organization in Washington dedicated to promoting better understanding of Africa.

THE NEW AFRICAN AMERICANS

Family ties and tribal ties and the land itself are the most binding forces in life for Africans. They may be driven away by war or famine, but not many will leave because they want to." The minister-counselor paused again, then added, "Perhaps younger Africans are beginning to feel differently, especially those who go away to study."

From my years in Ethiopia and Nigeria, I felt I knew what the minister-counselor was talking about. After I left his office that day, I remembered something an old storyteller told me when I visited the Eastern Region of Nigeria. It is a belief of the Ibo people that if a person leaves his village because of something he has done or simply because he wants to go away, he will always come back. He may travel or wander all over the world; he may try in every way not to come back, but someday he will return to his village and to whatever awaits him there. The Ibos call this belief "The Dance of Life."

Everything the minister-counselor said was true. African requests for immigrant visas do lag far, far behind those from other parts of the world. The present list of persons worldwide waiting for immigrant visas to the United States has 3,600,000 names on it. Of that total list only 69,000 names are African—less than 2 percent.

The family reunification law has strong congressional support because its humanitarian purpose of bringing families together is understood by all Americans. Furthermore, new immigrants with close relatives already in the country are almost certain to receive family support in adjusting to their new homeland.

But what about the immigrant visa applicants who cannot qualify under the family reunification clause? That would include most of the 69,000 African applicants on the immigration waiting

Beyond the Year 2000

list. A few might qualify under the "occupational and professional skills needed in the United States" clause of the immigration act, but the number admitted annually in that category is also severely limited. For immigrant applicants who cannot qualify under the family reunification or professional skills categories, the chances of visa approval are small.

In 1996 the first ray of hope appeared for many people who want to immigrate but who seem destined to wait for years or forever for visa approval. The U.S. State Department was authorized to organize an annual "diversity lottery" for areas of the world that traditionally have been low in immigration. Over one-third of the fifty-five-thousand visas available through the lottery—twenty thousand—were reserved for Africans. To enter the lottery you didn't need to have close relatives in America or be a doctor or engineer or some other kind of professional. All you needed was a high school education or two years experience in a skilled occupation—and a great deal of luck. To get an immigrant visa your name had to be one of the twenty thousand African names kicked out of the lottery computer at the National Visa Center in Portsmouth, New Hampshire.

Recently Jennifer and I went to one of the big hotels in Washington, D.C., for an interview and photo session. When we drove up to the hotel parking garage, a sign informed us that the garage was temporarily full. We were almost late for our appointment and sat there pondering what to do. Just then a young man in a garage-attendant uniform tapped on the window and told us to follow him.

"I will find you a place," he said.

THE NEW AFRICAN AMERICANS

It took him some looking on three levels, but he did find us a place and a good one near the elevator. I gave the young man a reasonable tip for his efforts, and when he thanked me, I thought I detected a familiar accent.

"Are you from Ethiopia?" I asked him, and he told me that he was.

Washington has probably the largest number of Ethiopians in America, and I asked him if he had family in the city. He told me that he did not, that he knew no one in Washington when he arrived a year ago.

That made me curious. "How did you get a visa?" I asked.

He smiled and said, "Diversity lottery."

So here was one of the lucky ones, the first one I had met. "Are you going to college?" I asked him.

"Next year," he said, "when I save money." He told me that he was driving a taxi at night.

"When do you sleep?" I asked him.

"In my taxi," he said. And then he added, "But I stay awake when I am driving."

Talking to the young Ethiopian made me feel that the diversity lottery is a good thing—that twenty thousand young immigrants like him couldn't be bad for our country. And talking to him reminded me of something else the minister-counselor had said to me the day I met with him. After talking about family reunification and professional skills as reasons for issuing immigrant visas, he said:

"Why could a certain number of immigrants not be accepted for the old reason, the original reason, that brought most immigrants to America: simply to try to build a better life for themselves? I am sure some means of selection could be found, and then more Africans could come."

Beyond the Year 2000

I don't know whether the minister–counselor is still in Washington, but I am sure, wherever he is, he thinks the diversity lottery is a splendid idea.

For all the reasons discussed here, immigration from Africa to the United States is unlikely in the foreseeable future to come even close to the levels of immigration from Latin America and Asia. But Africa is forever linked with America by history, people, and culture. Immigration from Africa, even in modest numbers, will add to the vitality and variety of our country while at the same time reenforcing the cultural contributions of the first African Americans and their descendants.

Additional Information About Africa

Africa is the second largest of the earth's continents. With an area of 11,677,240 square miles, it is more than three times the size of the United States, including the states of Alaska and Hawaii. The population of Africa (1998) is estimated to be 763 million, as compared to a United States population of slightly over 270 million. (The population of the vast Asian continent is over 3.5 billion, of Latin America—including Central America, South America, and the Caribbean—500 million).

There are fifty-five countries in Africa. Seven are in North Africa (largely populated by Arab, Berber, and Egyptian people). Forty-eight countries are in sub-Saharan or "black" Africa (Africa below the Sahara Desert). The size and population of African countries vary widely. A number are quite large. The Democratic

Additional Information About Africa

Republic of Congo (formerly Zaire) is one-fourth the size of the United States. Ethiopia is almost three times the size of California. Nigeria is about the size of Texas and Oklahoma combined. Other comparisons: Ghana is slightly smaller than Oregon; Liberia and Indiana are about the same size. Only a few African mainland countries are quite small; The Gambia is 4,363 square miles, Equatorial Guinea, 10,830 square miles. Even so, The Gambia is twice the size of Delaware, and Equatorial Guinea is ten times larger than Rhode Island!

The present-day national boundaries of most African countries were determined in the nineteenth and early twentieth centuries by European countries that seized African land and established colonies. The main colonial powers were Great Britain, France, Belgium, and Portugal; Italy and Germany also tried unsuccessfully to establish colonies. The purpose of colonialism was to exploit the natural resources of Africa and to establish markets for the products of European countries. A long smoldering resentment of colonial rule began to burn in all African countries after World War II. Beginning in the 1950s African countries, one after the other, threw off the yoke of colonialism, both by peaceful means and, when necessary, through violent confrontation. By the 1970s all African countries had gained their independence.

Although not the largest country in terms of land area, Nigeria, with 114 million people, is by far the most heavily populated African nation. Other African countries with large populations are Egypt, sixty-five million; Ethiopia, fifty-eight million; the Democratic Republic of Congo, forty-nine million; South Africa, thirty-nine million. A principal reason for Nigeria's large population is that one-third of its land is arable (suitable for growing crops), a much

THE NEW AFRICAN AMERICANS

greater percentage of arable land than in any other African country. Much of Africa's terrain is desert, rain forest, and mountains.

Africa's population is divided into several thousand distinct ethnic groups, each with its own language, customs, and beliefs. Sudan, for example, is estimated to have as many as six hundred different ethnic groups; Nigeria, four hundred; Ghana, one hundred. Many of Africa's ethnic groups are quite small, some only a few thousand. Other ethnic groups are large. For example, the Amhara of Ethiopia number twenty-two million; the Akan of Ghana, eight million; the Kikuyu of Kenya, five million. In a number of cases large ethnic groups reside in more than one country. The Hausa people, thirty-nine million strong, live mainly in northern Nigeria, but large numbers of Hausa are citizens of the neighboring countries of Niger and Cameroon. The Nyanja, an ethnic group of ten million, live in three East African countries: Malawi, Zambia, and Zimbabwe. The breakup of large ethnic groups into different countries is a legacy of European colonialism when countries were created arbitrarily without regard to territory occupied by ethnic groups (or tribes, to use the term of that era).

Just as there are thousands of ethnic groups, so are there thousands of African languages or dialects of the same language. Almost one hundred languages are spoken by one million or more Africans. Swahili, a Bantu language, is spoken by fifty million Africans in Kenya, Uganda, Tanzania, and the Democratic Republic of the Congo.

In a holdover from colonialism, European languages have been retained as official languages in a number of African countries. English is the official language in Ghana and Nigeria, French in Senegal, Portuguese in Mozambique. These European languages

Additional Information About Africa

are the languages of government and the languages of instruction in secondary schools and colleges. In many cases ethnic languages are used in the elementary schools. The vast number of languages have led to problems of education and communication in many African countries.

The African continent has a wide range of natural resources and agricultural crops that help finance governments and provide employment for many of the people. Among the most important of these natural resources and crops are gold, diamonds, petroleum, uranium, timber, cocoa, coffee, and palm oil. South Africa is the world's largest producer of gold; Côte d'Ivoire the world's largest producer of cocoa, Ghana the third largest. Nigeria is the world's sixth largest producer of petroleum. Diamonds, both precious gems and industrial diamonds, are found in commercial quantities in several countries, among them South Africa, Sierra Leone, and the Central African Republic. Kenyan and Ethiopian coffees are considered among the world's best.

While these natural resources and export crops are important, they only partially meet the economic needs of most African countries; and only a very few countries in Africa—most notably South Africa—have any appreciable manufacturing or industrial base. The majority of people throughout Africa depend on subsistence-level agriculture for a living. In Kenya, for example, 75 percent of the labor force is engaged in agriculture, 80 percent in Ethiopia, 86 percent in Malawi, 75 percent in The Gambia, 54 percent in Nigeria. In all of sub-Saharan Africa only South Africa has less than 50 percent of its labor force engaged in agriculture. According to United Nations' studies and other national and international research organizations, most African countries are among the poorest in the world.

AFRICAN TRIBAL SCULPTURE

At their best, traditional African tribal woodcarvings, primarily the masks and statues of West Africa and Central Africa, are among the world's most powerful art. Indeed, Pablo Picasso declared that African sculpture "has never been surpassed." Early twentieth-century European artists profoundly influenced by African sculpture make an awesome list which includes such names as Matisse, Picasso, Modigliani, Derain, and Brancusi.

Only a few thousand pieces of African art that was originally used for tribal religious purposes exist today. Most were collected by missionaries and anthropologists working in Africa in the late nineteenth and early twentieth centuries. After that time very little African art was carved for truly tribal ritual use. Fortunately, examples of this great art can be found in a number of American museums such as the National Museum of African Art in Washington, D.C., the Los Angeles County Museum of Art, and the Metropolitan Museum of Art in New York. Great African tribal art collections can be seen in the British Museum, the Musée de l'Homme in Paris, and in other European museums.

Many African craftsmen today carve copies or reproductions of masks and statues that were once used for tribal ritual purposes. Some of these carvers are quite skilled, and their work makes interesting decorative art. To experience the power of true African tribal art, however, it is necessary to visit a museum with African art holdings or look at some of the many excellent books about African tribal art now available.

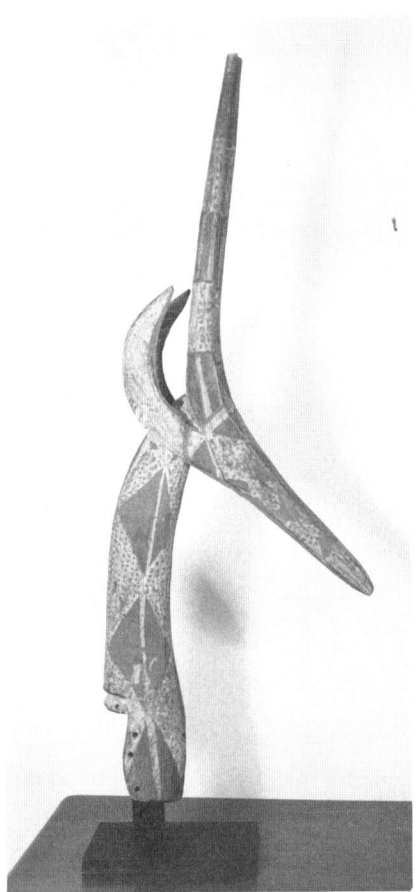

Above: Antelope headdress once used by dancers of the Kurumba tribe, Burkina Faso (formerly Upper Volta), in mourning ceremonies. Upper right: Dance mask representing a beautiful maiden, once used by Bajokwe tribe, Angola. Lower right: Dance mask, M'Pongwe tribe, Gabon, once used in funerary and initiation ceremonies.

THE NEW AFRICAN AMERICANS

In a curious contrast to the dominance of agriculture, Africa has many large cities. Five cities in South Africa have between one and two million people. Addis Ababa, the capital city of Ethiopia, has a population of over two million, as does Nairobi, Kenya. Abidijan, the administrative capital of Côte d'Ivoire, has almost three million people. Lagos, Nigeria, and its surrounding metropolitan area have an astonishing population of almost eleven million, making it one of the most populous urban areas in the world. A number of other African cities are in the one million range. The growth of African cities has been going on for decades as people have streamed from impoverished villages to urban centers hoping for a better life. Some have found a better life, but most face continual unemployment and exist as occasional manual laborers, peddlers, servants, or beggars. The unemployment rate, principally urban unemployment, of most African countries is unknown. Where it is known, it ranges from 10 percent (Ghana) to 50 percent (Djibouti). Nigeria has an unemployment rate of 24 percent, Kenya of 34 percent. By comparison, the unemployment rate in the United States in recent years has been below 6 percent.

Health conditions in most African countries are cause for great concern. Malnutrition is widespread. Famines in Ethiopia in the 1970s and 1980s killed an estimated one million people. Infant mortality is very high. Of every one thousand babies born in Africa, ninety-one die before their first birthday. The infant mortality rate for the entire world is fifty-eight per thousand. For the United States it is seven per one thousand.

Today Africa bears the brunt of the AIDS epidemic. Figures released by the World Health Organization in 1998 showed that of over thirty million persons worldwide infected with HIV, the virus

Additional Information About Africa

that causes AIDS, twenty-one million live in Africa. The United States Agency for International Development, the World Health Organization, and other international assistance organizations are helping Africa fight this frightening problem.

Since throwing off the colonial yoke and achieving independence, most African countries have gone through years, in some cases decades, of bitter internal conflict as different ethnic groups strove for power. Bitter civil wars have raged in Sudan, Angola, and Liberia for many years and are still raging. Terrifying genocide tore Rwanda apart. In the 1960s the Ibos of the Eastern Region of Nigeria tried unsuccessfully to secede and establish a separate country to be called the Republic of Biafra; the result was a bloody and costly conflict known as the Biafran War. In the Horn of Africa, the Ethiopian province of Eritrea struggled for decades to establish itself as a separate country. Finally in 1993 Ethiopia recognized Eritrea's sovereignty. In many other African nations brutal and corrupt dictators have seized power and abolished all civil rights.

The political picture in Africa is not entirely bleak, however. Some countries have solved or lessened their ethnic problems and have successfully ridded themselves of dictators. Among these countries are Côte d'Ivoire, Senegal, Ghana, Mozambique, Malawi, Uganda, and Kenya. The indigenous black population of South Africa has overcome the evil of apartheid—the strict segregation of and discrimination against native Africans by whites—and a government is being established that will allow the races to live together peacefully.

In March 1998 President Bill Clinton made an eleven-day, six-country trip to sub-Saharan Africa. It was the first visit to Africa by

THE NEW AFRICAN AMERICANS

an American president in office, and its purpose was clearly to influence how Americans think about Africa and how Africans think about America. The president began his visit in Ghana, a symbolic choice since Ghana was the first of black Africa's European-ruled colonies to achieve independence in 1957. Ghana is also the first African country to have one of its citizens, Kofi Annan, named Secretary General of the United Nations.

In Accra, Ghana's capital, the president, Mrs. Clinton, and their party, were met in Independence Square by a huge crowd estimated at over a quarter of a million people, by far the largest gathering President Clinton had ever spoken to. In his speech the president predicted "the beginning of a new African renaissance."

"For centuries, other nations exploited Africa's gold, Africa's diamonds, Africa's minerals," Mr. Clinton said. "Now is the time for Africans to cultivate something more precious: the mind and heart of the people of Africa through education.

"A decade ago, business was stifled," the president continued. "Now Africans are embracing economic reforms. Today from Ghana to Mozambique, from Côte d'Ivoire to Uganda, growing economies are fueling a transformation in Africa."

In addition to Ghana, President Clinton visited Uganda, Rwanda (airport stop only), South Africa, Lesotho, and Senegal. The stay in South Africa was the longest on the trip and the only one designated as a state visit. President Clinton left no doubt that he and his advisers believe that a stable and economically healthy South Africa can help other sub-Saharan African countries in their development. President Clinton had long private talks with South Africa's idolized president, Nelson Mandela, and when he spoke to the South African National Assembly, Mr. Clinton said:

Additional Information About Africa

"Now the courage and the imagination that created the new South Africa and the principles that guide your constitution inspire all of us to be animated by the belief that one day humanity all over the world can at last be released from the bonds of hatred and bigotry."

Bibliography

Apraku, Kofi. *African Emigres in the United States: A Missing Link in Africa's Social and Economic Development.* New York: Praeger, 1991.

Ashabranner, Brent and Russell Davis. *The Lion's Whiskers and Other Ethiopian Tales.* North Haven, CT: Linnet Books, 1997.

Ashabranner, Brent. *Still a Nation of Immigrants.* New York: Cobblehill Books, 1993.

Bial, Raymond. *The Strength of These Arms: Life in the Slave Quarters.* Boston: Houghton Mifflin Company, 1997.

Branch, Muriel Miller. *The Water Brought Us: The Story of the Gullah-Speaking People.* New York: Cobblehill Books. 1995.

Charles, Nick. "Closing the Door," *Emerge,* July/August, 1995.

Chicoine, Stephen. *A Liberian Family.* Minneapolis: Lerner Publications Company, 1996.

"Diverse Hispanic Population to Become Largest U.S. Minority," *Population Today,* November, 1997.

Goss, Linda and Marian E. Barnes, eds. *Talk That Talk: An Anthology of African-American Storytelling.* New York: Simon and Schuster, 1989.

Haley, Alex. *Roots: The Saga of an American Family.* New York: Doubleday & Company, 1976.

Haskins, James. *Black Dance in America: A History Through Its People.* New York: Thomas Y. Crowell, 1990.

———. *Black Music in America: A History Through Its People.* New York: Thomas Y. Crowell, 1987.

Mama, Raouf. *Why Goats Smell Bad and Other Stories from Benin.* North Haven, CT: Linnet Books, 1998.

Bibliography

Millman, Joel. *The Other Americans: How Immigrants Renew Our Country, Our Economy, and Our Values.* New York: Viking, 1997.

———. "Out of Africa—Into America." *The Washington Post*, October 9, 1994.

Pawlak-Seaman, Susan. "Remembering the Past—the Cape Verdean Immigrant," *The Standard-Times*, New Bedford, MA, February 2, 1997.

Potter, Joan and Constance Claytor. *African-Americans Who Were First.* New York: Cobblehill Books, 1997.

Rawley, James A. *The Trans-Atlantic Slave Trade.* Toronto: George J. McLeod Limited, 1981.

Stroebel, Ken. "Folk Tales from Africa." *The Norwich Bulletin.* Norwich, CT: February 10, 1998.

Zeinert, Karen. *The Amistad Slave Revolt and American Abolition.* North Haven, CT: Linnet Books, 1997.

Index

(Because African countries and peoples are mentioned throughout the text, only specific entries are indexed here. *See also* general entry for Africa.)

Achuko, Blessing, 76
Achuko, Chibuike, 79
Achuko, Chigozie, 79
Achuko, Kelechi, 79
Achuko, Ogechi, 79
Achuko, Olivia, 73–80
Achuko, Sam, 73–80
Africa
    agriculture, 95
    arts and crafts, 36–38, 96–97
    cities, 98
    colonialism, 29, 93–95
    countries, 92–93
    ethnic groups, 94
    health, 98–99
    languages, 94–95
    political turmoil, 99
    population, 94, 98
    size, 92
African-Expression Gallerie, 36–37
African folktales, 14, 64–69, 70–72

African immigrants today
    educational status, 29, 31, 35
    numbers, 30
African music, 13–14, 24
African students in the U.S., 31–32
American Colonization Society, 24
AIDS, 98–99
Angola, 41, 97, 99
Annan, Kofi, 100
Apartheid, 99
Awusah, Emmanuel, 79

Benin, 35, 36, 37, 66–68
Biney-Amissah, Albert Jeffery, 56–57
Biney-Amissah, Elizabeth, 56–57
Biney-Amissah, Naana, 56
Biney-Amissah, Theodora, 56–57
Biney-Amissah, Thomas, 56
Borquaye, Adeline, 34
Borquaye, Amanda, 34
Borquaye, Iris, 34

Index

Borquaye, Seth, 32–34
Borquaye, Yolanda, 34
Branch, Muriel Miller, 65
Burkina Faso, 97

Cameroon, 94
Cape Verde, 24, 25–26
Central African Republic, 95
Chambers, Hannah, 4, 6, 8
Chicoine, Stephen, ix
Clinton, Bill, 99–101
Comoros, 27
Congo, Democratic Republic of, 41, 93
Côte d'Ivoire, 25, 95, 98
Creole, 53–55

Davis, Fussell, 64
Djibouti, 98

Egypt, 93
Equatorial Guinea, 25, 93
Eritrea, 99
Ethiopia, 26–27, 93, 95, 98, 99

Food, 48–53

Gabon, 97
Gambia, The, 6, 8, 93, 95
Gambia River, 6
Ghana, 23, 32, 93, 94, 95, 98, 100

Haley, Alex, 3, 6, 8

Ibo, 55, 60, 62, 88, 99

Immigration Act of 1965, 20
Immigration and Naturalization Service, 31
Immigration to U.S.
   African percentage of world total, 84–85, 88–89
   diversity lottery, 89
   early restrictive legislation, 17–18
   family reunification, 85, 88
Isusus (savings clubs), 55
Iweogu Favour, 62
Iweogu, Okechukwu (Chuck), 60–63
Iweogu, Uche, 62

Johnson, Florence, 53–55
Johnson, Thomas S., 53–55

Kelechi African Authentics, 73, 78
Kenya, 27, 95, 98, 99
Kouabena, Jocelyne, 86
Koukoui, Elie, 35–38
Kunta Kinte Heritage Festival, 3–8
Kwanzaa, 4, 6

Liberia, 23–25, 41–42, 93, 99
The Lion's Whiskers (Ashabranner and Davis), 64, 70

Malawi, 94, 95, 99
Mama, Cherifath, 69
Mama, Raouf, 60–69
Mandela, Nelson, 100
Miller, Augustus, 43
Miller, Deazee, 43

Index

Miller, Francis, 41–44
Miller, Kau, 43
Miller, Nya, 86
Miller, Pearl, 41–44
Miller, Thomas, 43
Monteiro, Flavio, 87
Mozambique, 94, 99
Munthali, Mwiza, 87
Museums with African art collections, 96

Nigeria, 23, 74–75, 93–94, 95, 98, 99

Opara, Anthony F., 49
Opoku, Bernice, 39
Opoku, Harry, 38–40
Opoku, Mondell, 38–39
Opoku, Zulema, 38, 39
The Other Americans (Millman), 58

Pipim, Peter, 84

Refugees, 39, 41
Restaurants. *See* Food
Richmond, Va., 58
Roots (Haley), 3, 8
Rwanda, 41, 99

Sao Tome and Principe, 27
Selassie, Haile, 27
Senegal, 25, 94, 99
Sierra Leone, 52–53, 95
Slaves and slavery (in the Americas)
    Brazil, 10
    Caribbean Islands, 10
    Cultural contributions, 12–14
    Freedom struggles, 14–15
    North America, 10–11
South Africa, 27, 93, 95, 98, 99, 100–01
Storytelling. *See* African folktales
The Strength of These Arms (Bial), 15
Sudan, 41, 94, 99
Swahili, 94

Tucson, Ariz., 50

Uganda, 99
United Nations, 44, 95, 100
U.S. Agency for International Development, 99
U.S. Census Bureau, 29
U.S. Congress, 41

Voice of America, 41–42

Washington, D.C., 48–52, 58
The Water Brought Us (Branch), 15
Welbeck, Elnora, 28
Welbeck, Paa-Bekoe Henry, 28
Weyone ("We Own It") Foods, 52–55
Why Goats Smell Bad (Mama), 67–68
World Health Organization, 98–99

Yao Loko, 4, 5

Zambia, 94
Zimbabwe, 94